Simply Rodgers and Hart

The Music of Richard Rodgers and Lorenz Hart

21 of Their Most Popular Works

Arranged by Matt Hyzer

Simply Rodgers and Hart is a collection of the most famous songs by Richard Rodgers (1902–1979) and Lorenz Hart (1895–1943). They have been carefully selected and arranged by Matt Hyzer for Easy Piano, making many of Rodgers and Hart's most enduring melodies accessible to pianists of all ages. Phrase markings, articulations, fingering, pedaling and dynamics have been included to aid with interpretation, and a large print size makes the notation easy to read.

Rodgers and Hart worked together as a songwriting team for over 20 years and wrote some of the world's favorite musicals, including *Babes in Arms*, *The Boys from Syracuse*, *Pal Joey*, and many others. Richard Rodgers was one of the most prolific and popular American composers, having written more than 900 songs and over 40 Broadway musicals. For these, he won numerous awards including an Oscar, Grammy, Emmy, Tony, and Pulitzer Prize. Lorenz Hart tragically died young (at 48), but was known for his sophisticated lyrics, which spanned a broad range of emotions and raised the standard for Broadway songwriting. His collaborations with Rodgers have become favorite selections among singers, instrumentalists and audiences, young and old, around the world. For these reasons and more, the music on the following pages is exciting to explore.

After all, this is *Simply Rodgers and Hart!*

D1571696

Illustration by Sarah Vaughan

Alfred

Contents

Bewitched, Bothered and Bewildered

Words by Lorenz Hart
Music by Richard Rodgers
Arranged by Matt Hyzer

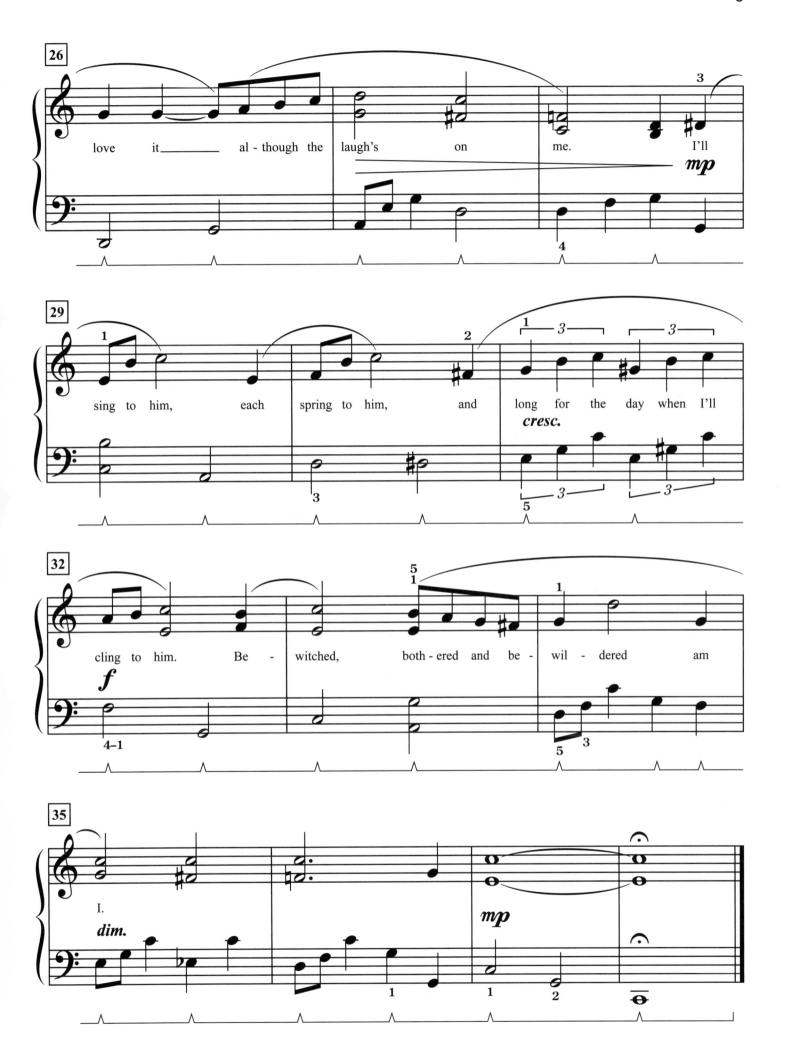

Blue Moon

Music by Richard Rodgers
Lyrics by Lorenz Hart
Arranged by Matt Hyzer

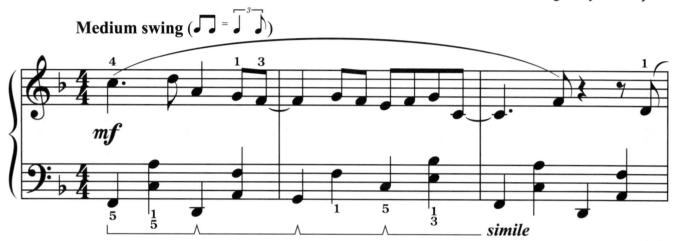

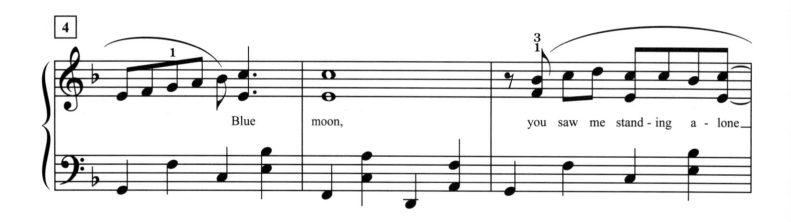

Blue moon, you saw me stand-ing a - lone

with - out a dream in my heart,

And then there sud - den - ly ap - peared be -

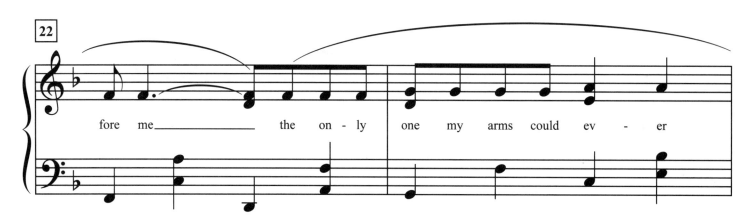

fore me_____ the on - ly one my arms could ev - er

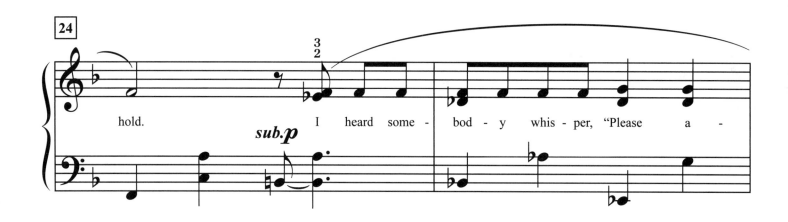

hold. I heard some - bod - y whis - per, "Please a -

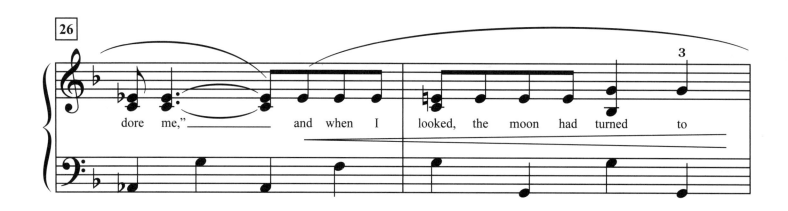

dore me,"_____ and when I looked, the moon had turned to

The Blue Room

Words by Lorenz Hart
Music by Richard Rodgers
Arranged by Matt Hyzer

Moderately

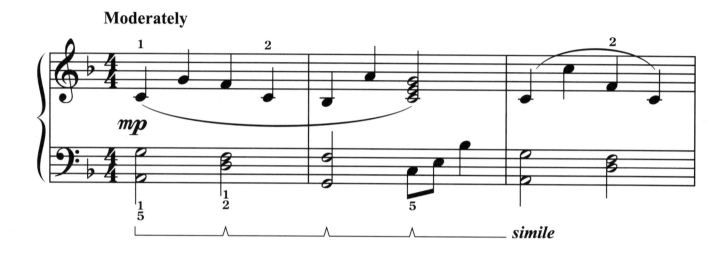

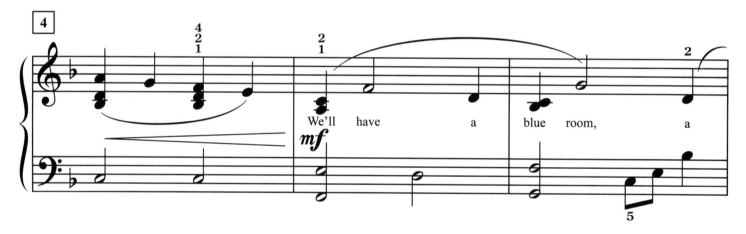

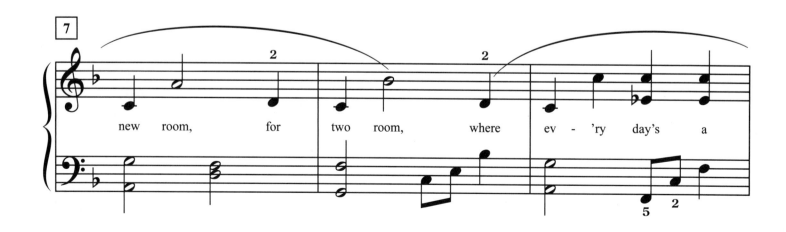

12

30 trous - seau, and Rob - in - son Cru - soe is

33 *f* not so far from world - ly cares _____ as our

35 blue room far a - way up - stairs. *mp*

37 *rit.*

Dancing on the Ceiling

(He Dances on My Ceiling)

Words by Lorenz Hart
Music by Richard Rodgers
Arranged by Matt Hyzer

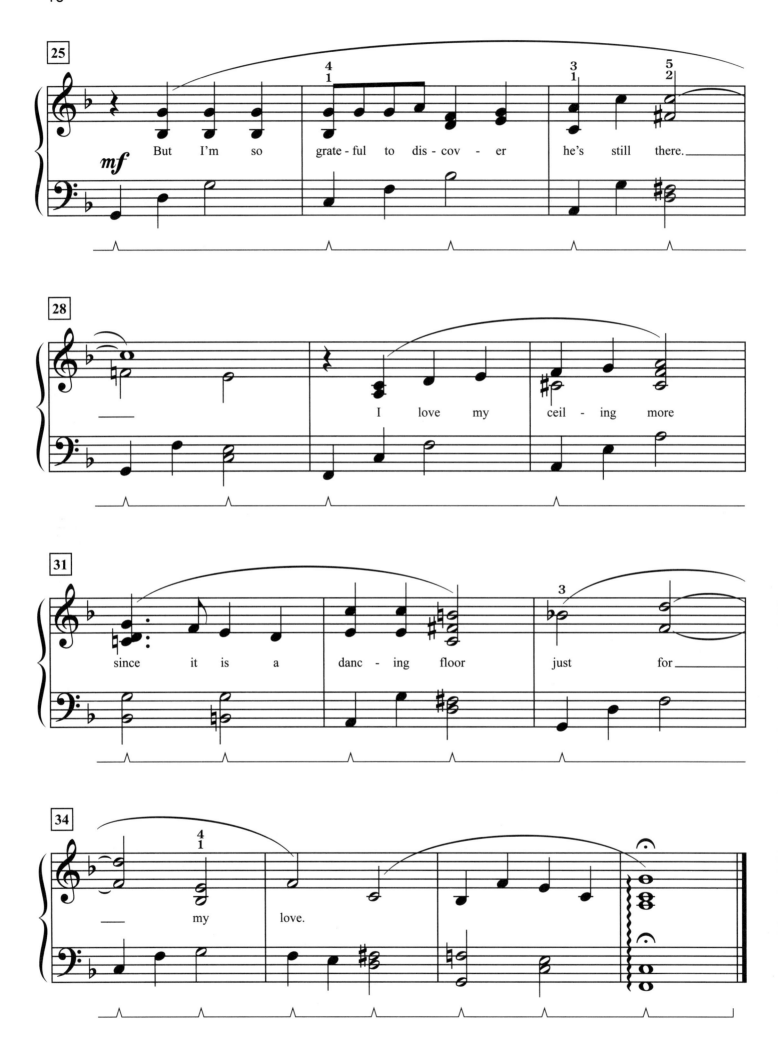

Have You Met Miss Jones?

Words by Lorenz Hart
Music by Richard Rodgers
Arranged by Matt Hyzer

Falling In Love with Love

Words by Lorenz Hart
Music by Richard Rodgers
Arranged by Matt Hyzer

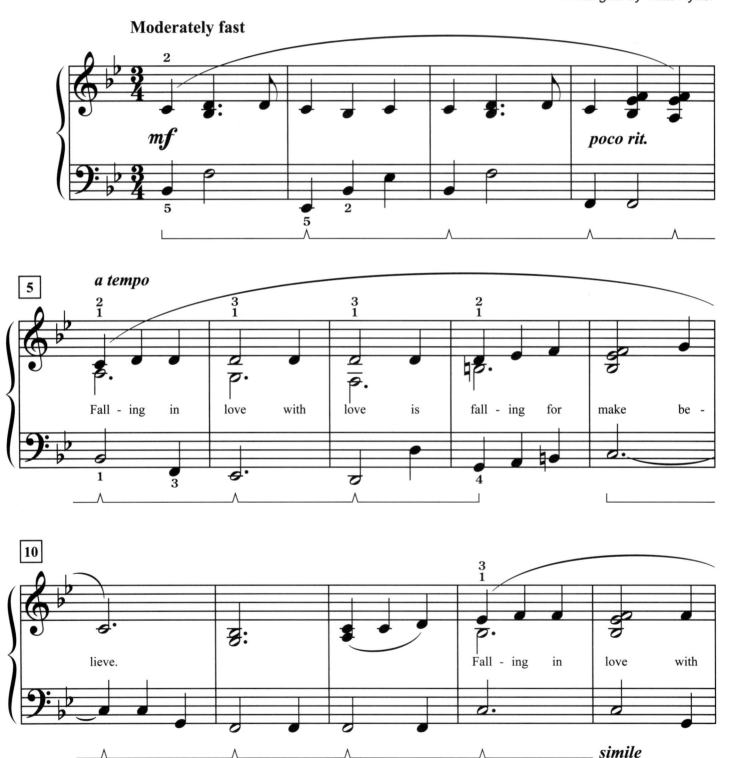

love   is   play - ing   the   fool. _____

Car - ing   too   much   is   such   a   ju - ve - nile

fan -   cy. _____

Learn - ing   to

trust   is   just   for   chil - dren   in   school. _____

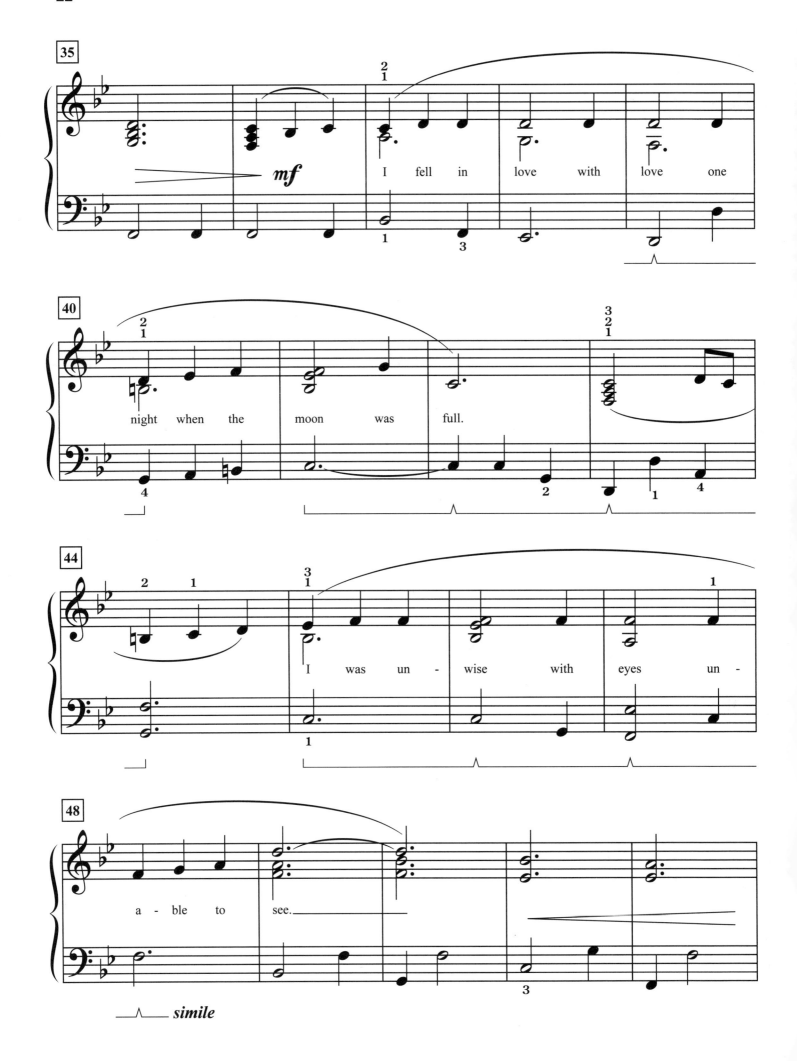

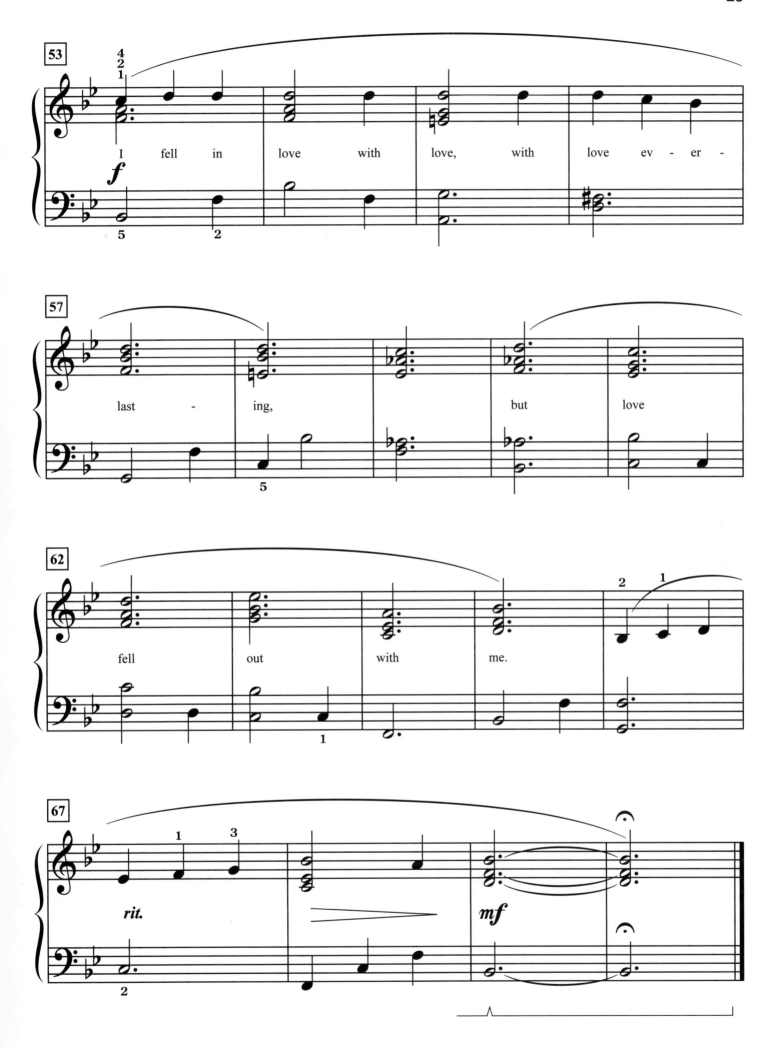

He Was Too Good to Me

Lyrics by Lorenz Hart
Music by Richard Rodgers
Arranged by Matt Hyzer

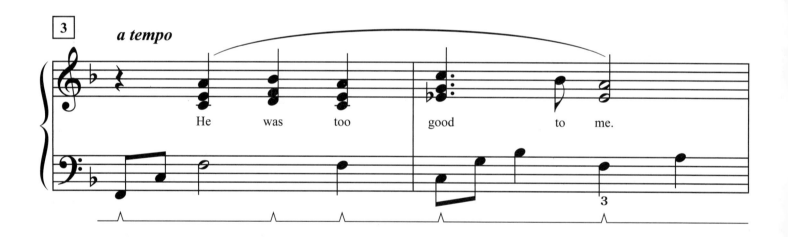

He was too good to me.

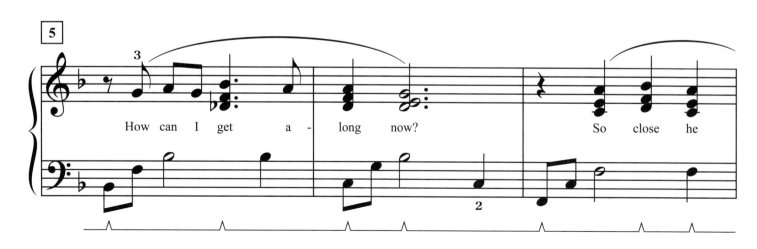

How can I get a - long now? So close he

26

When I was mean to him

he'd nev-er say, "Go 'way now."

I was a queen to him.

Who's goin' to make me gay now?

I Didn't Know What Time It Was

Lyrics by Lorenz Hart
Music by Richard Rodgers
Arranged by Matt Hyzer

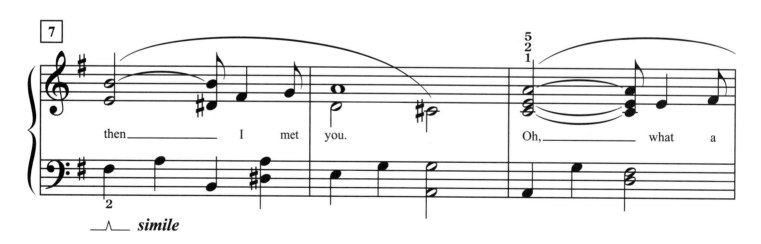

I Could Write a Book

Words by Lorenz Hart
Music by Richard Rodgers
Arranged by Matt Hyzer

I Wish I Were In Love Again

Words by Lorenz Hart
Music by Richard Rodgers
Arranged by Matt Hyzer

It Never Entered My Mind

Words by Lorenz Hart
Music by Richard Rodgers
Arranged by Matt Hyzer

Once I laughed when__ I heard you say - ing

42

Mountain Greenery

Words by Lorenz Hart
Music by Richard Rodgers
Arranged by Matt Hyzer

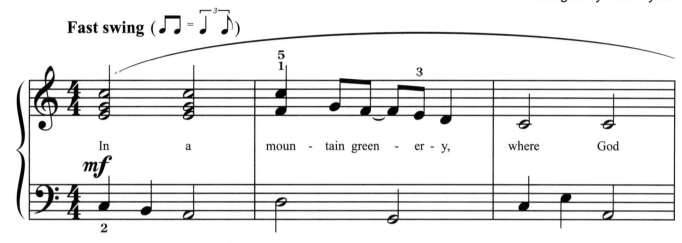

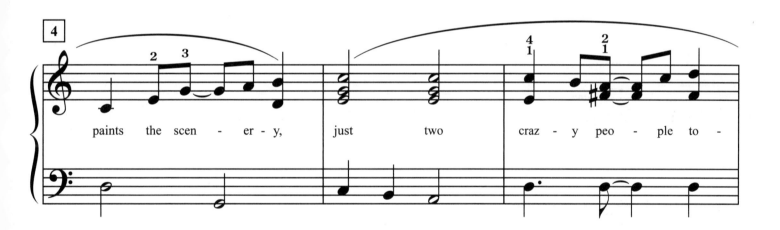

The Lady Is a Tramp

Words by Lorenz Hart
Music by Richard Rodgers
Arranged by Matt Hyzer

Johnny One Note

Words by Lorenz Hart
Music by Richard Rodgers
Arranged by Matt Hyzer

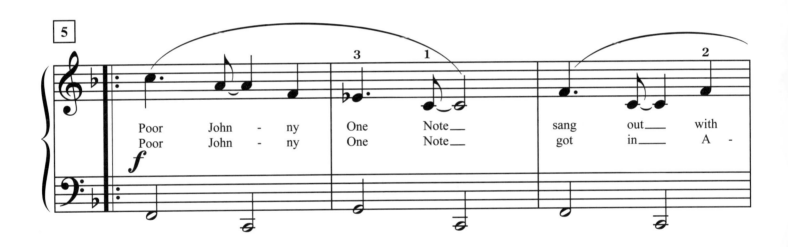

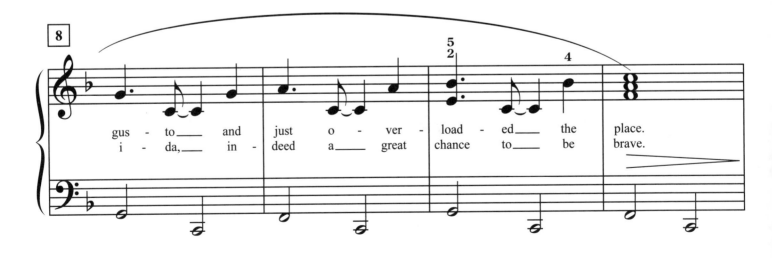

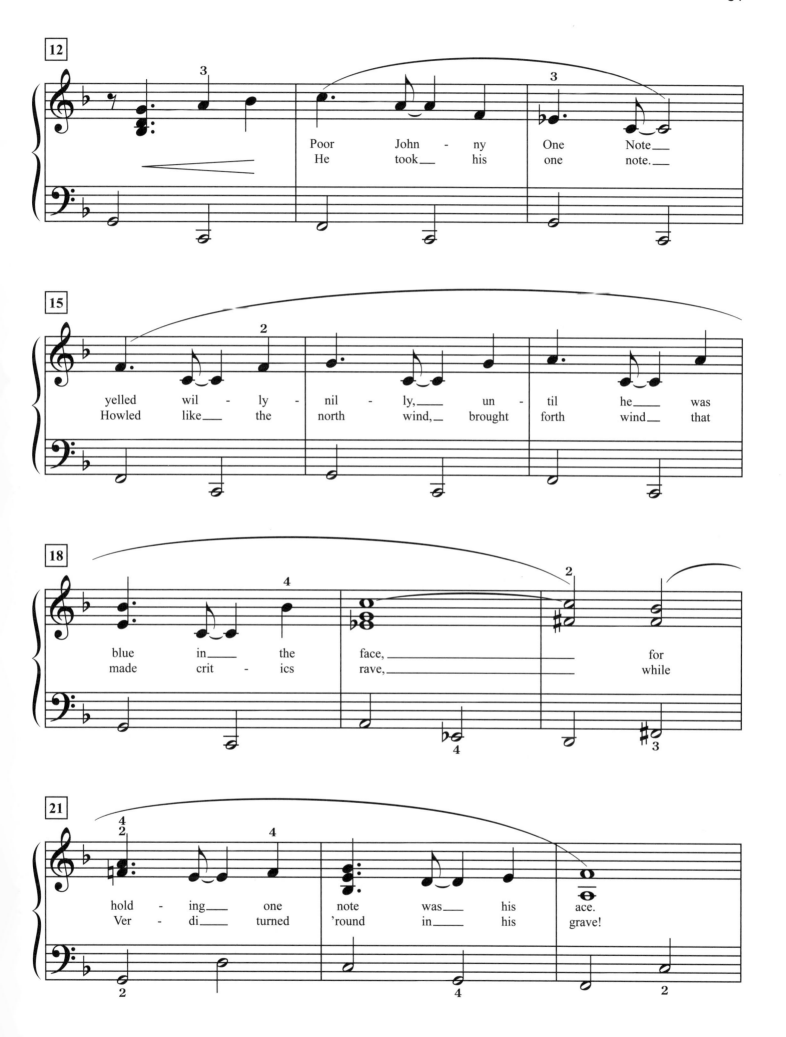

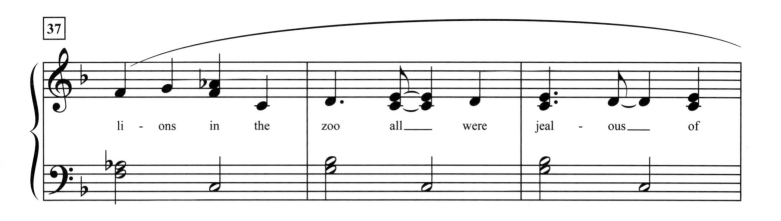

li - ons in the zoo all___ were jeal - ous___ of

John - ny's___ big trill. Thun - der - claps

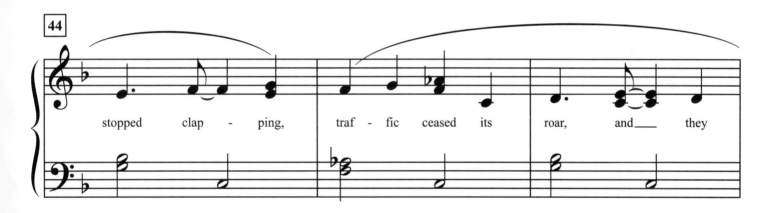

stopped clap - ping, traf - fic ceased its roar, and___ they

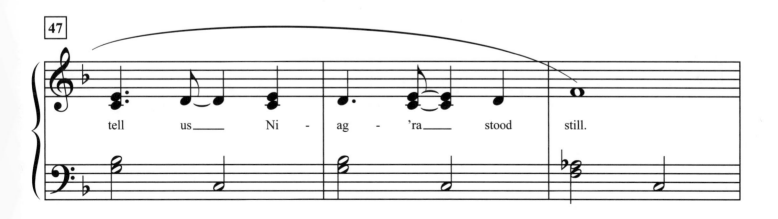

tell us___ Ni - ag - 'ra___ stood still.

54

55

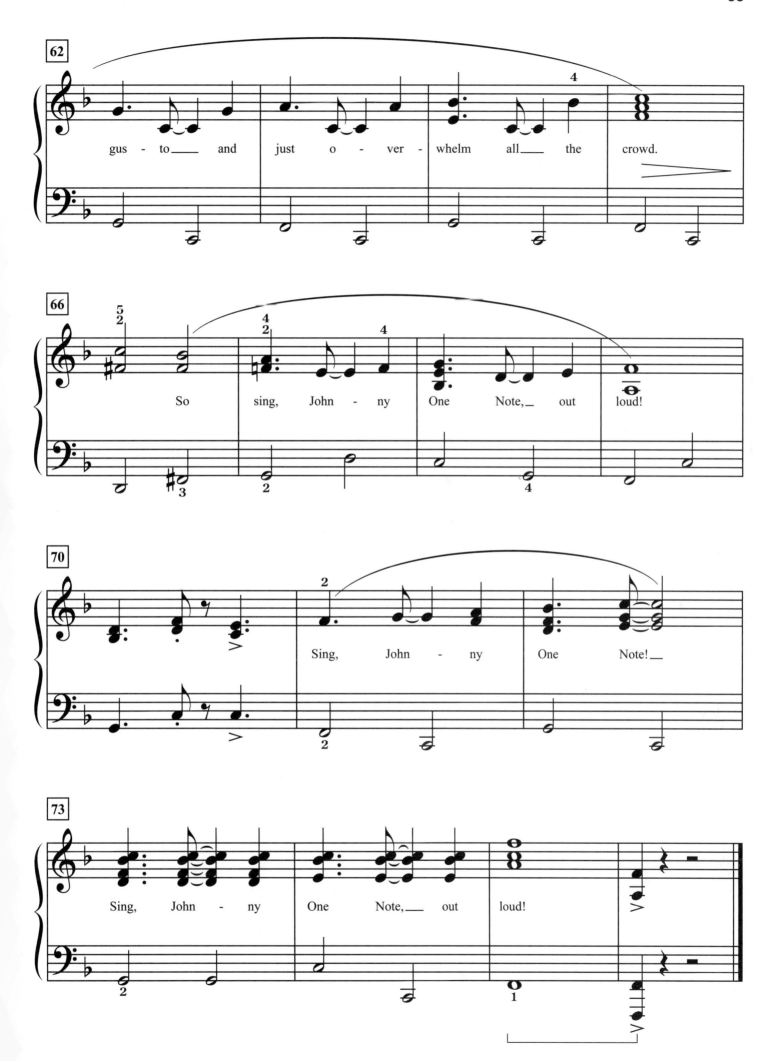

My Funny Valentine

Words by Lorenz Hart
Music by Richard Rodgers
Arranged by Matt Hyzer

My Heart Stood Still

Words by Lorenz Hart
Music by Richard Rodgers
Arranged by Matt Hyzer

There's a Small Hotel

Words by Lorenz Hart
Music by Richard Rodgers
Arranged by Matt Hyzer

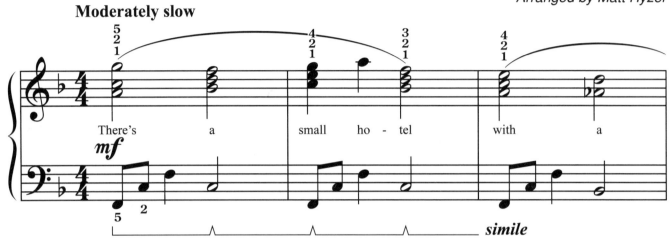

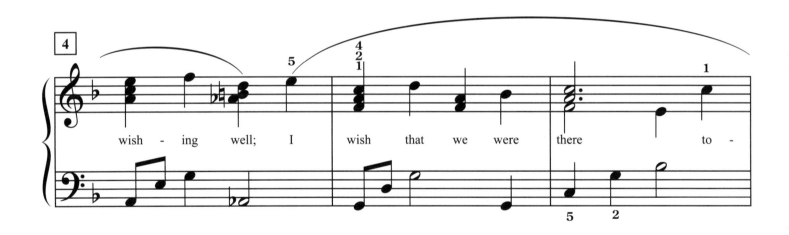

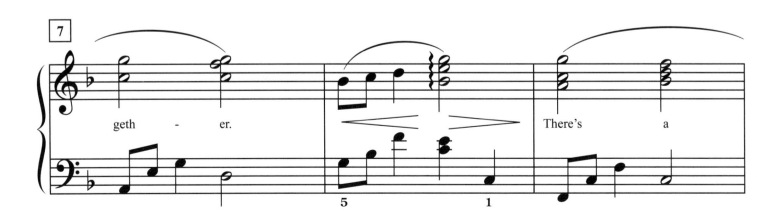

You Are Too Beautiful

Words by Lorenz Hart
Music by Richard Rodgers
Arranged by Matt Hyzer

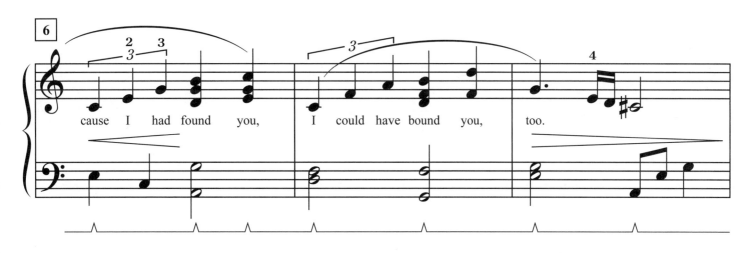

Where or When

Words by Lorenz Hart
Music by Richard Rodgers
Arranged by Matt Hyzer

Moderately slow

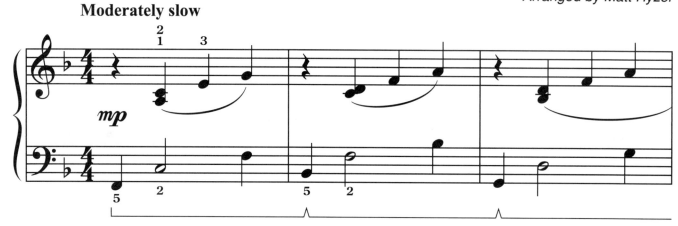

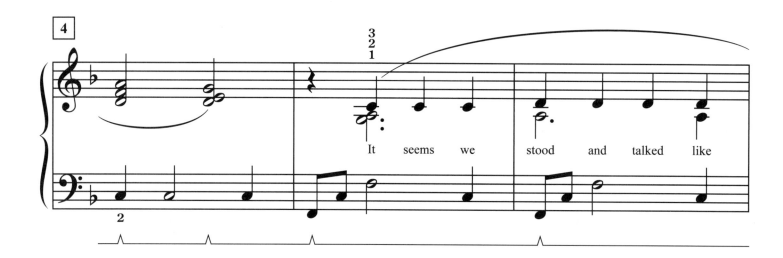

It seems we stood and talked like

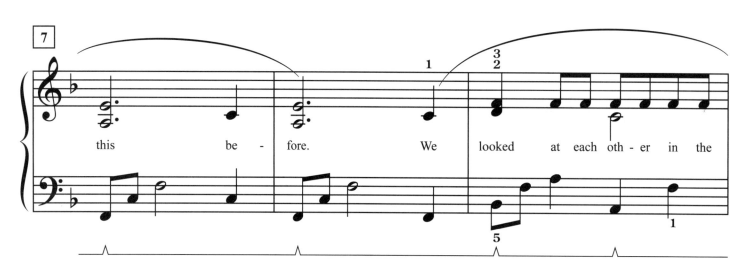

this be - fore. We looked at each oth - er in the

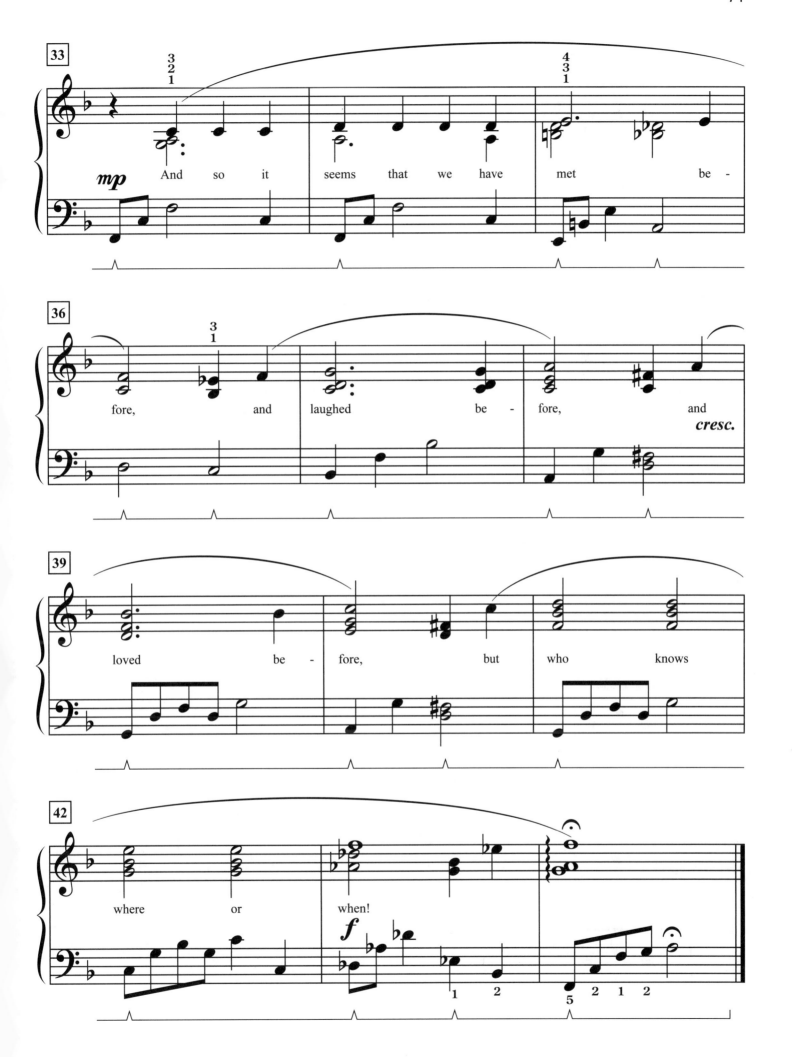

With a Song in My Heart

Words by Lorenz Hart
Music by Richard Rodgers
Arranged by Matt Hyzer

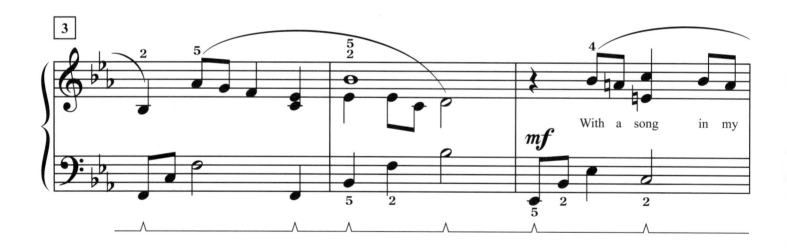

74

You Took Advantage of Me

Words by Lorenz Hart
Music by Richard Rodgers
Arranged by Matt Hyzer

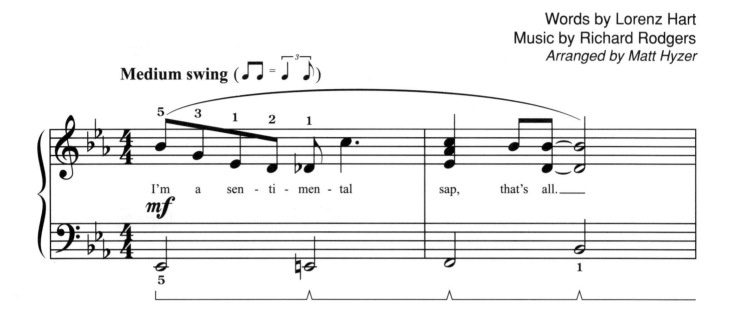

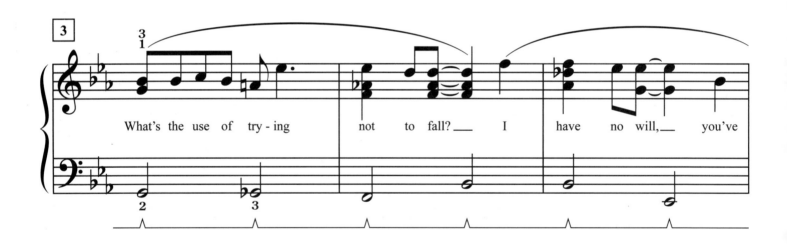

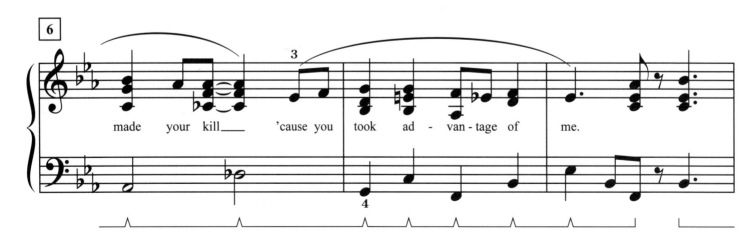